Putter and the Red Car

A Cross-Country Family Adventure

Kate K. Lund

Illustrated by Ana Maria Velicu

First edition 2015
Published in the USA by Kate K. Lund
Paperback ISBN: 978-0-9971516-2-6
eBook ISBN: 978-0-9971516-1-9

This book is dedicated to my husband,
boys and Putter.
May we always share in such
epic adventures!

Hi. My name is Putter. I am a seven-year-old Airedale terrier and this is my red car. I love going for rides in my red car with my family.

One day, Mom said we were going on a very long drive. Dad got a new job and we were moving to Seattle, Washington from Boston, Massachusetts. Oh boy! A super long car trip with my family – I was so excited. Ruff! Ruff!

Our first stop was in Sturbridge, Massachusetts. This was my very first time staying in a hotel and I wasted no time making myself comfortable!

The next day, we left early for Pennsylvania. It was a long drive, but I was so happy with my head out the window and the wind in my face.

When we arrived at our hotel, the first thing my brothers and I did was play on the playground. After sitting in the car all day, it felt great to run around outside!

When we were good and tired, Mom called us in for dinner and quiet time before bed.

The next morning, we packed up the red car and left for Chicago. I was super excited because my friend Hercules lives there and we were going to visit him.

We arrived at Hercules' house and I could hardly wait to get out of the car. I was so excited to see my buddy! Before I knew it, we were playing chase at top speed around Hercules' yard. Hercules is strong, but I run faster.

Soon, it was time to go to our hotel for the night, and guess what? I got to ride in an elevator for the first time ever! I even got to push the button to make the door open. I love new experiences!

The next morning, we were off again in the red car – headed for Sioux Falls, South Dakota. The drive was long so I slept a lot. We stopped for lunch and I had a hamburger!

On the way to Sioux Falls, we planned to visit a place called Mount Rushmore which is a national monument with the faces of four United States presidents carved into a mountain.

But there was a problem. It started to rain very, very hard. When we got to Mount Rushmore, we could not see anything through the windows of my red car. I was disappointed, but Mom and Dad said we could come back another time so I felt better.

It felt good to finally arrive at our hotel for the night. I was so tired from all that driving and all that rain that I found myself a nice soft spot, fell fast asleep and dreamed of the adventures ahead.

The next day, we were off to Buffalo, Wyoming. On the way, we stopped at a museum with real tipis and I decided to go inside one. It was a bit dark and scary at first, but it was exciting to explore a real tipi.

By this point, we were getting closer and closer to our new home in Seattle. Only two more days to go!

Montana was our next stop. The scenery became more and more beautiful. I just loved looking out the window. I have never seen so many mountains.

After another long day on the road, we arrived in Missoula, Montana. We checked into our hotel and Mom took me for a walk. Everybody wanted to say hi to me. I love people!

After our walk, we went out for dinner. It was great because I was able to sit with my family. Even though moving all the way across the country felt a little scary, as long as I am with my family, I am happy.

Finally, the day arrived! This was the day we drove to Washington State and our new home. Boy was I excited! After driving for six days and more than 3,000 miles, we were in Seattle. It was the experience of a lifetime, and I am so glad I was able to share it with my family.

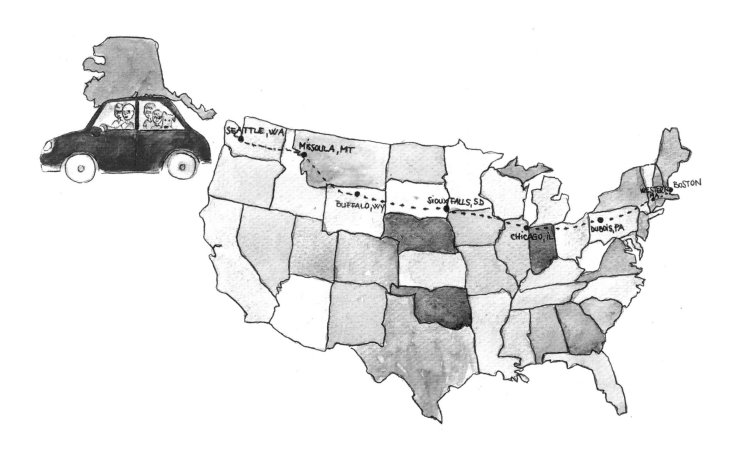

The End

About the Author

Dr. Kate Lund is a licensed clinical psychologist who writes and speaks on a variety of topics aimed at empowerment and the development of one's true potential. Putter and the Red Car is the first in a series of books for young children linking a life-long passion for Airedale terriers with such ideas as adaptation to change, building resilience and the power of possibility. Dr. Kate lives in Washington State with her husband, two boys and lively Airedale.

CPSIA information can be obtained at www.ICGtesting.com
Printed in the USA
LVIW01n0002160216
475278LV00007B/9